The Squaw with Blue Eyes

Marybeth Weston

Shank Painter Company, Inc.
Provincetown, Massachusetts

Cover: *Comanche War Party, Mounted on Wild Comanche Horses*, 1834-37,
by George Catlin
courtesy of the National Museum of American Art, Washington, D.C.

Other books by the author:
Poems: *Silk from a Spool* (Kaleidograph)
Poems: *Underside of Leaves* (Kaleidograph)
House & Garden's 26 Little Gardens (Viking)
Decorating with Plants (Pantheon)

The Squaw with Blue Eyes
The story of Cynthia Ann Parker

History/American Indians
A one-hour one-character play

Drawings on pages 1 and 4 by Angel de Cora

Library of Congress catalog card number 87-126368
ISBN number 0-9619658-0-0

Printed by Shank Painter Company, Inc., Provincetown, Mass.
    First Printing: 1986
    Second Printing: 1987
    Third Printing: 1995

2

3

The Squaw with Blue Eyes is the true story of a pioneer Texas girl who was captured by Comanches and became the mother of a great Indian chief. Her name was Cynthia Ann Parker.

This story of a lost child, who became a strong woman, is part of the history of the American West. It is also a testament to enduring family love.

The narrative is written to be read aloud or performed with simple costume changes and Comanche flute music. The author has used fictional techniques but has tried to be faithful to the known events and dates—and to conversations with some of Cynthia Ann Parker's kin. Anglo and Indian, divided by blood and the spilling of blood, they came in time to consider themselves one family, proud of their double heritage.

The Squaw with Blue Eyes

The time:	Late 1863
The place:	The front porch of a log cabin in east Texas

A woman wears a long buckskin-colored dress and a bright shawl. Near her, on a ladder-back chair, are a girl's sunbonnet; leather Indian collar, beads and headband; and a frontier woman's sunbonnet and apron. She leans forward and speaks in a calm defiant manner.

Yes. I am Cynthia Ann, the squaw-woman—the Parker's girl who lived with Indians. Oh, I know what your neighbors say about me.

Removing her shawl, she beckons her visitors toward the porch steps and whispers:

Lived up by the Red River as a savage.
Had an Indian baby!
Sullen, didn't want to come home.
Her folks caught her three or four times trying to escape.
Tried to ride back to the Indians!

I know what they whisper. But sit a spell. I'll try to tell you how it really was.

Cynthia Ann returns to her past in memory and almost in appearance. Dreamily, she puts on a girlish sunbonnet. Her voice, at first, is almost childlike.

7

At our log fort that May morning–it was 1836–I had helped my mother after breakfast and was looking for my brother John. I was 9; he was 6. Mother was hanging clothes, with little brother Silas and baby Orlena at her side. It was a pretty day. Most of the men were working in the fields, and the gate to the stockade was open.

All at once, Indians came up on horseback. Someone called out from the watchtower. Cousin Rachel tried to slip out to call the men in the fields.

The Indians gazed down at us from their ponies, gazed at our light hair and blue eyes. We wondered at their lances, their black eyes, their hair straight as arrows.

Arrows! Arrows fly over their shoulders as hundreds of Indians gallop through the open gate. "Cynthia Ann!", my mother cries, her voice small in the sound of horses' hooves, screams, and the crackle of gunfire. "Cynthia Ann!" I remember–outstretched hands, holding on to what other hands would take. I remember– things I do not want to remember: Mother and grandmother were running and calling. I saw my grandmother fall.

And then–an Indian scooped me up, another took my brother John. They carried us away with Elizabeth Kellogg and Rachel and Rachel's little boy James Plummer. That night, far from the log fort, they made a fire and danced, terrifying us with their drums and shouts and shadows. I remember the drum beats, heartbeats, the women's shrieks–and then a long, long sleep.

Next morning they wrapped our hands and feet with rawhide, strapped us on horses' backs. I saw the women and my little cousin James carried away by other Indians. I never saw them again.

For days and days we traveled westward. The sun burned our skin. They gave us strong strange meat I could not eat. A young brave they called Nawkohnee, Peta Nocona, did not let us out of his sight. I whispered to my brother John: We are good for a ransom. Horses, or maybe gold. I did not tell him I wondered: Where can Mother and Father be? Are they captives too?

At a river crossing, another tribe of Indians bartered for John and took him away. Little Johnny, a wailing pink six-year old. I cried all night, with no one to comfort and no one to comfort me. I knew my worth now. Not a gold ransom but to be some Indian's slave.

The prairies that spring were covered with bluebonnets. I remembered my mother's blue-and-white apron. The plains were blurred patches of yellow flowers, lavender, and red. I thought of her patchwork quilts.

Westward, beyond four mounds, beyond mesas and ridges I could not count, on a flat high prairie we came to a village of tipis, noisy with dogs and children.

Women peered at my dusty clothes and shucked me out of them like an ear of corn.

Remembering this, Cynthia Ann pulls off the sunbonnet and shakes out her hair.

A thin ear of corn, too little to be of much use.

But one woman gave me food and set me to gathering twigs and buffalo chips for a campfire. Later, by a shallow river where willows and women wash their hair, she bathed me, and dressed me in their way, and took me to her tent to be her child.

Saying this, Cynthia Ann puts on a leather collar, transforming her buckskin-colored dress into Indian clothing.

I still remembered a Bible verse Mother had taught my brothers John and Silas and me: Be ye kind, one to another, tender-hearted, forgiving each other. Could I ever forgive Indians for taking me? And God for letting me be lost?

I wriggle when the women part my hair in the middle with a quill. I sulk when I am given an Indian name, Naduah, and handed a baby to mind while its mother scrapes buffalo hides. I watch young girls pound new leather to soften it for moccasins. I see painted men making tools from bone. Naked children chase dogs away from racks of drying meat, and sometimes they chase and throw things at me. Like some little animal I am silent by day, whimpering by night.

But I work. I look for the kindest faces. I grow strong. After awhile, I begin to listen for words to repeat to myself until I can say them aloud–like a Comanche.

They call themselves the People. They rule all the land that they can see, wherever they are on horseback. Always they set their tents to face eastward to greet the sun. Sometimes I am the first to wake and would peer from the tent flap and remember the wagons that brought us to Texas from Illinois, the ox-teams of relatives and belongings. My grandfather was a preacher and our leader at Parker's Fort, our settlement on the Navasota River near–, near–, and in time I could not recall the names anymore.

I still remembered my father reading to me. Listening to Grandfather and Uncle Daniel preach and say blessings at table. And that I ate with a shiny fork. Oh, I would have howled our hymns off-key with coyotes, loud across the plains, if I had known my blue-eyed kin were searching for me.

But gradually that life faded to a dream.

I am the south wind's little sister; my skin grows coppery. The west wind is my brother; my feet are never still. I know every child and every flower and bird by its Comanche name. Toh-tsee-ah, flower. Pia-huu-tsu, bird. I have a pony to ride. I play the children's games, and I learn the game to help the men find buffalo.

Tell us, horned toad,
Little lizard with horns like a buffalo,
Tell us, shiny cricket,
Tiny creature dark as the buffalo,
Tell us, dark crows flying,
Broad-backed birds, quick as the buffalo,
Where are the buffalo roaming today?
Horned toad, run away!
Cricket, hop away!
Crows, fly away!
Where you go, we will go—
And there we'll find the buffalo.

Never a day was the same. We would come and go with the grass and seasons, following the animals and stars. Comanches are the most daring horsemen of the plains. Comanches are like swifts, the birds that speed through the air and can feed and even sleep while flying.

In summer we would pound a paste of wild grapes and plums to eat with dried strips of meat, foods to eat on horseback without stopping to make a fire. Comanches want no more belongings than they can wear, or carry in blanket rolls on double poles the dogs and horses pull.

By the light of the great September and October moons, when the blue quail and bobwhites break from tall grasses, and antelope bound from dancing yellow trees, we would find buffalo herds moving southward and have great feasts around our leaping fires.

After five September moons, I am fourteen, taller than most of the other girls. I learn more of the ways of women. No more can

I run with children, dodging among tent poles and riding the tamest ponies. Now I soak bark to tan leather. I cook. I help make tents. I embroider clothing with beads, as spring and summer stitch the brown earth with flowers.

Remembering these days, Cynthia Ann slips a bead necklace over her leather collar and speaks as a full-grown Indian woman.

Often we would meet Comancheros, the Spanish-Mexican traders from New Mexico who came from the west in creaking wooden carts to trade with us. They bought our buffalo robes, and brought us metal arrows and cooking pots, red cloth, tobacco, and beads. We spoke some Spanish then.

One day, white traders came from eastward. They talked of guns, of towns, of gold. I knew many of their words! One trader stares at and follows me, though I walk with lowered eyes. The man catches me by the arm. He spins me about, looking long into my face. He calls to another man. I try to break away and cannot. His blue eyes stare into mine. "A squaw with blue eyes!" he mutters. He holds up one of the mirrors he barters, and I stare at my blue eyes.

The young brave, Peta Nocona, runs to me and tells me to hide. He grabs the mirror and flashes it, to bring others to his side. He sends away the traders with their blankets and knives, buttons and shells. He tells me he will not let the white men take me away.

All the tribes that I had seen—Comanches and Kiowas and Apaches, Shoshones, Wichitas, Wacos, and Caddoes—and the Spanish and Mexicans, all had dark eyes. So do most animals and birds. Even the wolf and the owl have eyes like embers, not blue. I wondered, were my birth people those people? Or sky people? Ice people? And all the others the brown-eyed earth people the Great Spirit made and loves? If it had not been for the feathers of bluejay, and the blue flowers that spatter the prairies with blue rivers and lakes, I would have felt more ugly and alone.

The trees leaf out once again, and another year passes. I watch the young braves with their high cheek bones and their strong arms like gliding eagles. If one is meant for me, I will know it when his eyes speak to me, and if my tongue dares to speak to him.

I look at Nocona, now the young war chief of the tribe called Nawkohnee, the Wanderers. His words, like his arrows, are direct and bear his own sign. Other men listen. He is a chief, but young men are not born chiefs. They become that through vision and daring. Nocona had made his journey into the wilderness before I knew him—to ponder the ways of the eagle and serpent, to listen to the spirits, to find his own sign. Four times the moon must rise for a Comanche boy alone, without food or water, while he asks for guidance and vision. His home will be as far as he and the People can see—each day wherever they are—and he must see clearly and far.

With other members of the tribes I watch young braves show off for girls, do trick riding and roping, dance and prance with their lariats and lances, and strut and preen in new feathers—drumming like prairie chickens at mating time. We laugh at the showing off, but I am wistful. Why do I dream of Nocona? I have no warrior father or brother to be his brothers. And I am still a troublesome child to him, and blue-eyed.

Yes, I knew the men could be cruel to women not their own. White women, Mexican. If I had not been a child when I was taken, I would not have hoped for any man's kindness. I have seen captive women cower, and heard their cries. And I knew even a chieftain's wife must share her husband with other wives, if she is childless, or if he chooses.

But, I look at Nocona.

One evening I walk in my softest moccasins past a riverbank where he sits playing a flute he carved of red cedar.

He is playing a courtship song. Is he playing the song for me?

I sit far away. Does he know I choose to be chosen? Will my thoughts leap the distance between us?

The sound of the flute trembles on the summer air. The moon shines on the rocks of the river crossing. And he walks over to me.

But a warrior rides into our camp that night and tells of an Apache plan to attack us from the west. The young men are eager for war. Without captured horses, how can they barter for wives? The braves put on their black war paint and uncover their shields of buffalo hide.

Nocona comes to the tent of the barren woman I help and live with now. They talk. He promises only that he will come back when the battle is over.

I know some in the tribe will say: She was not born of our People. She is not for Nocona.

I see it in his mother's eyes: The girl with blue eyes chooses you. Must you choose her? You can have any wife.

I see it in his father's eyes: Spirits, counsel him well, for the good of my son, and the People.

While we wait for his warriors to return, I make willow baskets to fetch roots and berries for his mother and grandmother. I search for acorns and pecans, feathers and flints. I think of Peta Nocona leading his men. Does he think of me? I dread the dangers he faces, and sing a song a mourning dove teaches me.

Cynthia Ann hums a phrase of the dove's mournful song, and says:

> Hear how the mourning dove
> Weeps for her only love,
> Evening and morning she cries.
>
> Though some may scorn her love,
> Hear how she mourns her love,
> Walking with downcast eyes.
>
> Lonely the mourning dove
> Weeps for her only love—
> Fallen to earth in front of her eyes.
>
> Hear how the mourning dove
> Weeps for her only love,
> Morning and evening she cries.

But just when I had lost all hope, Nocona is safely home!

We mourn for the braves we lost. We bury our dead, covering them in crevices where they sit to face a new sunrise. We howl to the skies.

> Who will bring the children food?
> Who will bring the old ones food?
> We are so few on this vast plain.
> We are lost if our young men die.
>
> Only the sun and moon will remain.
> Only the sun and moon.

After the time of mourning, Nocona walks slowly to my tent. His voice is deep and sure. He wants me. Thinks I will do. Thinks I will do what is right for him—and right for me!—and not just what any firewood woman or captive anybody's-wife will do.

He leads a string of horses to my tent. He brings a gift of many horses to my tent.

If his mother and father still are troubled by the girl with blue eyes, they are wise enough to honor his wisdom now. They make me welcome. And the women dress me as a bride.

Cynthia Ann exultantly puts on more beads and a ceremonial headband.

Squaw. What an ugly word that is. Only Anglos say it. Squawk. Squat. Squabble. Nocona said I was his Wa-i-puu, woman. His true-eyed, blue-eyed woman for life.

You do not think I was a wife.

We shared no ring of gold or lamplight, and what we knew was love, some here libel lust. Yet I was a bride like any other bride— and as unlike as all brides are. We chose each other, not for the strangeness in our eyes but for the matched selves that recognized each other deep in the marrow of our bones—red marrow, white bones—like any other.

New to each other, we rode in the cool of the night, miles and miles by horseback by moonlight, and made our camp by a river to sleep till noon, wrapped in our blanket and each other's arms. We would wake and bathe in the long afternoons in the dappled shade of cottonwood groves. No other blue eyes had seen this land. I tell him:

> I rejoice in and praise
> The length your bones have chosen,
> The hidden paths your blood takes.
> I rejoice in and praise
> The skin that clothes you,
> And the shy hair curling like ferns.
> I praise the pale nails of your hands and feet,
> Shells that border the restless tides of you.
> I praise your words, your thoughts
> That outrace the winds.
> Your path I choose
> Forever.

On hunting trips we ride side by side, proud before the others, and I carry his lance and shield. We are not servile, we Comanche women. Chosen by my choice, I am no more settled down than a deer or wildcat. I am free to ride with Nocona.

No sidesaddled, corseted, meek women we, but women who show our feelings, even anger! I tell Nocona a woman without a temper is a landscape without weather. I could make Nocona laugh. He could not stay angry with me.

Closing her eyes, Cynthia Ann remembers as if in a dream:

He embroiders me with silver thread to make for us sons and daughters to wear his silver after we are dead. Comets in the darkness of the night return to darkness. But out of every starry path linking a man and woman, one star may be– destined– to make its own new world.

And so in time I am heavy with child. And light of heart, I talk with other women heavy with child, and with the old ones heavy with years. The women say I am carrying a son, and marvel that I carry well. Comanche women, leaping on and off fast horses, making and breaking camp, often lose the blood that would have made the child they want, and the tribe needs. Our men are so often gone, or fall in battle, and we are not a people with the sound of many children running and laughing. Settlers have so many cubs, and we so few, I heard a warrior say. And they took young children, like Johnny and me, to bring up as their own.

My child grows big in me. I am like a slender moon with the old moon in its lap. I laugh. Soon my child will play hide-and-seek with me among the rocks, red and gray rocks wind-streaked as clouds.

Peta Nocona and I called our first-born: Quanah–fragrance–for our land of flowers. I pray that he will be a man of courage and wisdom, who will win much praise from the People someday. When he is born there is much gladness. His grandmother searches Quanah's face, his fingers, his toes, for any sign of blue-eyed strangeness. She finds none–though in time he is taller than most, and sometimes blue lightning flashes in his dark eyes!

Soon my son rides in his cradleboard as all of us on horseback gallop to new campsites. My baby is brave and does not break the night's stillness with loud cries.

But sometimes there are nights of fear–fear of our old enemies the Apaches and Tonkawas, fear of settlers, and fear in a dry year when the buffalo grow gaunt and we with them. We ask for rain.

> Rattle, dry seedpods!
> Scream out, raincrow!
> Smoke, fall earthward!
> Moon, wear a rainbow!

And a storm would come–leaping like a mountain lion. We would see the sky arching its back, spitting fire, and clawing jagged gashes in the clouds. Mostly I remember bright clear days and starry nights and great white clouds like herds of white buffalo. More moons go by and I am with child again, sewing with women, gathering up clothes we wash on the rocks near small waterfalls.

While we work, we listen to the meadow lark and mockingbird and watch the scissortail.

I watch the old ones search for plants. I watch how they make their cures and mysteries as they take care of our second newborn child and me.

Another strong son! We called him Pecos, for the river by a western campsite.

And in those days I learn:

> Wash cuts and stings—with yucca root.
> Heal scrapes and burns—with comforting aloe.
> Clear the head—with pine in a pillow or bark of willow.
> Mend sprains—with twigs of juniper and cottonwood bark.
> Stop bleeding—with pounded prickly-pear pads.
> Ease fever—with boiled young pokeweed.
> Soothe toothache—with broomweed.
> Cure infection—with moss.

We knew the good medicine. If only I knew now how to heal the new fevers, give breath to the dead! That magic leaf or root, I do not know.

Sometimes in mid-summer we would go beyond four sacred Medicine Mounds to camp in a cool canyon with thin waterfalls and sandy riverbeds bubbling with springs. To hide from the howling wind in winter, sometimes we would stay in that canyon, our tipis stretched along a winding river. Or we would chase the sun that slinks low in the time of snow, and move southward to Mexico.

But now, on rides past San Antonio, we cross stagecoach trails going ever father west. California gold fever makes many whites our enemy. Soldiers invade the land. More and more white men come. They muddy the rivers with their wagon wheels. They bring disease in their blankets. They begin to kill our buffalo, the black pools of buffalo that bubble up from below the plains, giving wealth and safety—buffalo meat and robes for warmth in winter, tipis for cool shade in summer, tools, shields for defense. How can the People live without buffalo?

Then settlers take the land with their guns. They plow and skin it, and call our home their home. So the braves overturn plows and barrels, burn houses, steal mules and horses—to take back their own.

And buzzards whirl like smoke above our ruined villages.

Pecos is still a little boy, too young to understand my tears. But to Quanah, I speak of our fears. I tell him what I know. While he is young there is so much to learn. In the heat of battle, what word will be heard? A man does not listen when his ears ring with his own power and the whirr and shower of other men's arrows.

Those who go far, I tell him, have winding roads, each day a new beginning. Ride away from reckless counsel. Make no promises you do not mean to keep. Have many arrows in your quiver, strong arrows of your own making, Quanah. Learn from the old ways, learn from the new, seek out what is best—for you, and the People.

But often I wondered, in the far tomorrows who will remember our words or joys or sorrows, or even our names? Yet my thoughts could not be sad thoughts only, for Nocona and I have two sons and soon the joy of a daughter. For her bright eyes and tiny hands, we call her Toh-tsee-ah, Flower. And for my three children— Quanah, Pecos, Toh-tsee-ah, I am prized by Nocona and the People.

Then one cold dusty day in the short days of December, our band dallied between the Red River and the Wichita on a creek where sandy banks showed the tracks of fat quail and deer.

The men and boys hunt. My handsome sons, bareback on their ponies, had practiced their riding. Laughing, they ride as Comanche and Kiowa braves do. Full speed, holding on with just one foot in the loop of a mane, they slide to the side and shoot arrows from under the neck of a galloping pony!

We women pack the meat from yesterday's kill. We prepare to leave for another camp next day. The buffalo are moving south. Their winter coats are thick and shaggy.

The first frost on slanted brown grasses surprises me with forgotten memories—white sleeves, white yarn on a grandmother's knitting needles—memories knit together in a second of flashing sun! Then—flashing guns, a whirlwind of dust and sounds of pounding hooves, cracking tent poles, and rapid gunfire.

I remember—once more—outstretched hands, holding on to what other hands would take.

I remember—my mother's voice lost in the sound of horses hooves and screams.

Quanah! Pecos! I cry as Texas Rangers and soldiers thunder into our camp. I leap on my grey pony, holding my daughter. I ride to find Nocona and my boys. I am overtaken, and a man pulls me down from my pony.

He catches me by the arm. He wheels me about and looks at my hair and face. I try to break away. He shouts the words I had heard before—A squaw with blue eyes! Afraid for my dark-eyed daughter, I lift her up to save her.

I search the horizon. Are my child and I the only ones left alive? I see many in the tribe, fallen, bleeding. Friends, servants. One leans against a tree and sings his death song. A ranger rides up and says Nocona's name. What is he saying? Does he say he killed Nocona?

We ride to the Clear Fork of the Brazos, to Camp Cooper. The soldiers' questions are in English. Mine, in Comanche. No one understands.

Did both my sons fly away? Both my strong young sons? Why have you made a captive of me? I have sons to mother. I am a chieftain's wife. Set me free!

The young Ranger Captain, Sul Ross, looks at me. He questions me. He pities me! He sits at a desk and writes letters.

A soldier's wife bathes me and my baby. The women cannot say my daughter's Indian name and call her Topasannah and Prairie Flower. They dress me in a white woman's dress, and beckon others in, to look at us.

Recalling this day, Cynthia Ann slowly takes off her headband and beads, and drops them on the seat of a chair. She speaks sadly as she ties on a long white apron.

An interpreter understands some of my words, but never understands me. I wail as Comanche women wail, wail like a wolf or coyote. I sit on the ground and wrap my arms around my knees and howl. Oh we grieve, we Comanches, not dabbing at our eyes with lace handkerchiefs. The men cut their braids and daub their faces with paint. The women cut their hair, slash the skin of their arms and breasts, and paint themselves with their own blood.

I grieve now. Shall I cut off a finger? I have seen women with stumps, mourning with a fingerbone the husband or child lost to them. Other women may wear black or tear cloth. Comanche women tear their own flesh.

Nocona, Nocona, I say to the sky, surely your are circling like some watchful eagle and will know when to risk our rescue. But the days go by in single file, slow in gray moccasins. The days go by, and the gray blankets on their shoulders bring no sleep and no escape.

The women try to talk to me. Their gestures seemed to say, as neighbor women still do: Drudgery, dirt, and long wanderings on horseback! Indian women are old before their time. Carrying children on their backs and putting up tipis, skinning animals, washing on river stones. The men nothing but savages, they insist, and the women struggling on without even the hope of heaven. You were saved from this.

I did not have the words then to say to them: What life is not hard? Here on the frontier, women carry children in their bellies and arms and help build barns. White women skin animals, and also plant crops and spin and wash clothes in ugly boiling pots. They work sun-up to sundown, separated by as many lonely fields as each man claims as his own.

Indians work together, always with others to laugh with. I see how your women feed the burial grounds with their young bodies. I see how the captive black women work, and must give birth to children not their husband's own. Slave or free, most women here are slaves to a man and the land and the weather.

Comanches move north and south together. The Great Spirit feeds and waters the herds and provides the birds needed for feathers and food. And Comanches are masters of a vaster kingdom than this.

After many days, a man with a tall hat and a white beard rides all the way to Camp Cooper from Birdville near Fort Worth, carrying a letter. He looks at me with searching, kind blue eyes.

Can it be?, he questions. Are you the one we looked for, for so long?

He is Colonel Isaac Parker. He speaks gently. He says he may be my uncle, says his niece's mother is dead now, says he could take me and my child back to his house, says I could see sister Orlena and brother Silas–

Cynthia Ann raises her head, and her eyes widen.

"Cynthia Ann?"

And at last my stillness like a rock breaks open, and tears flow from a lost blue spring. I point to myself.

"Cynthia Ann, Cynthia Ann. Me."

Uncle Isaac tells me we will ride in a wagon, toward the land of cedars, tall oaks and pines. East, where Fort Parker fell–

Twenty-four years ago.

He makes the wagon ready. The women try to comfort me. I guess from their cadence what they mean: Griefs mend, roads wend, mourning that stretches on too long breaks the will to live. I know! I said so to others by blood-marbled waters where we crept after battles and the last rattle of arrows and drums. I once comforted others their grieving would cease. Now I cannot comfort myself with words of peace, or comfort my little daughter.

Cynthia Ann puts on a woman's long-brimmed frontier sunbonnet. Her mind leaps from then—to where she is now, a Southern woman speaking to new neighbors.

Shall I go on? Will you hear the rest of my story?

I go to my kinsmen. They speak to me. They read to me. And they wait to hear me say: I am home. I am grateful. It was hard living in a different place, with a different race, a different God.

I cannot say it.

My sister and my relatives are good. They claim me as their own, and pray for me. But in their eyes, there is a stain in me that will not come out, even if they washed me by a river and beat me against rocks and spread me out to dry in the whitest sunshine. They see me sullied, mother of Indians, kin to heathens.

I hear my story their way.

When the Indians took Johnny and me in the Comanche raid, they took five, they killed five.

My father, Silas Parker, dead. My grandfather, Elder John Parker of Virginia, dead. Uncle Benjamin and the Frosts, father and son, our old friends, dead. All speared and scalped!

Grandmother was attacked and left for dead at the fort. Mother and Silas and Orlena slipped through a little gate leading to a spring. Later they all escaped to Fort Houston.

Elizabeth Kellogg and Rachel Plummer, not yet twenty, were taken—shamed and sold to still other tribes. They suffered fearsomely. General Sam Houston paid the ransom for Elizabeth—$150. They say her husband would not have her back. When Rachel was found nearly two years later, by fur traders in the mountains north of Santa Fe, she was half-crazed from her misery and from the loss of her little boy James. Our relatives say she also had a child in captivity, a white child, her husband's child, killed in front of her eyes because he cried so. She died within a

28

year of coming home, not knowing James would be ransomed, not daring to hope.

Some say my brother John was found, but would not come back— that he married a girl in Mexico he loved too much to leave. Some say he once visited me–I never saw him.

Indians killed five, and kept five, when they took me.

How my kinsmen hate the Indians!

It was the spring of battles at the Alamo and San Jacinto, when Texas became a nation in 1836, they tell me, when I was taken as a child. 1860 when I was found. It was the next year, when this north-south war began, when Uncle Isaac brought me back.

How many women are now like me, divided between two families divided by war, grieving for men who hold the guns and men they may hold no more. Now the frontier forts are empty of soldiers. I am moved always father east, father back into the woods. No chance for Nocona and my sons, if they still live, to find me, or for me to send word to them.

I hear women speak of husbands and sons, dead or missing. I think of mine. Dead? Missing? Missing me?

I look out at these dark shaggy-headed trees that eat the sunshine. Here no coyote yips, sings his melody, chuckling with the nighthawk and Nocona and me. No antelope stops in his tracks before leaping white-tailed through clattering rocks. Walls and fences block out the sunrise. Even the long shadows of summer stumble over porch steps.

> Hear how the mourning dove
> Weeps for her only love,
> Evening and morning she cries.
>
> Though some may scorn her love,
> Hear how she mourns her love—

My days are full, though they feel empty. I am well, though I am like a dry river bed no river rushes through. When Nocona was a footfall away from me, I was still a supple girl in his arms through the long unlanterned nights. Now I am no one's delight, an extra mouth to feed, I and my daughter.

I am clumsy in a kitchen. My hands are like mud turtles, blundering and confused. Little glass things break in my hands. I can cook, but not your way. I sew, but not your way. In this house I chop wood, braid whips, spin thread, yet I feel like an old woman sipping a ladle, rocking a cradle, singing lullabies. I am like the blue chicory flower that fades to a ghost when it is cut from its place on earth.

And my daughter, Toh-tsee-ah, Prairie Flower, who rode on my back like an arrow in a quiver, a bright-eyed black-tufted arrow, is so ill. Ill with a fever I cannot heal. The medicine I know is far away.

My kinsmen say: She will get well if we pray hard enough. But even if God takes her, promise you will not give up and die, as some Indians know how to do, folding their arms, going when they are ready to.

But I have died many times before. And those who would mourn me already mourn me or have gone before.

I died to my childhood when I was a child and was captured and no one came after me. I died to my womanhood when I was a woman and saw my tribe dragged down to the dust and was recaptured. I will die to my motherhood if as a mother I can mother my young no more.

For myself I can die once more. I have held my daughter for such a little time, this baby who will never age. Many flowers will grow, come and go, but this one even in an endless field of flowers I would know.

I have no dread of afterlife. We shall ride across broad plains in the continuing soft breathing and purpose of God to a new place, perhaps with a trace of far memory of where we were before. Or, wrapped in the earth's shawl, we will sleep at the earth's breast. A new adventure? Or rest? Both are good, and I am not afraid.

I am at the rimrock of another land, a place where we are understood and understand. But—

———————————▶

Cynthia Ann tugs off her bonnet in a surge of hope.

Are my young sons laughing as they used to laugh? Leaping on their ponies and riding free? Are they sitting near Nocona, curled at his knee, listening to stories he could tell them of me? There the land is as open as the bright blue skies, and home is as far as anyone can see, and my People—all my people—will ride together. Proud. And free.

She stands tall and smiling.

31

Afterword

Cynthia Ann Parker, born in Illinois in 1827, died at her sister's house in east Texas. Legend has it that she pined-away in 1864 after the death of her daughter. A census and her gravestone suggest she survived at least until 1870–ten long years of being twice a captive and an outsider, ten years of hoping to rejoin the Indian husband and sons she never saw again.

Comanches say Nocona survived the ambush near the Pease River where she was recaptured. They say Nocona searched for her, wept, and died within a few years of a wound. Pecos died young, probably of smallpox. Quanah grew up to become war chief of the elusive Quahadi Comanches, the last on the southern plains to surrender. In 1875, after defeats by buffalo hunters and Indian hunters, he led the remnant of his tribe out of Texas's Palo Duro canyon to Fort Sill, Oklahoma. Indians already on the reservation and Col. Ranald S. Mackenzie who had pursued him for years, received this tall, half-white chief with curiosity and respect. He had never signed a treaty, never broken a promise, and no one had been more determined to keep his followers free.

When Chief Quanah learned his mother's Anglo name, he renamed himself Quanah Parker. He treasured a painting of her and Prairie Flower copied from an 1861 photograph. He learned English. He became a rancher, a judge, and part-owner of a railroad. He traveled ten times to Washington, D.C. on behalf of Comanches, Kiowas, and Apaches. He became a friend of Theodore Roosevelt and of prominent families in ranching history: Charles Goodnight, Dan Waggoner, Burk Burnett, W.S. Ikard and others. Cynthia Ann's family helped found the Baptist Church in Texas; Quanah founded the Native American Church.

The men in Cynthia Ann Parker's story are well remembered. In Texas, the town Nocona is named for her husband, the town Quanah for her son, Parker County for her Uncle Isaac, Fort Parker—a state park—for her grandfather and his family, and Sul Ross University for the young Texas Ranger, Lawrence Sullivan Ross, who found her and who became a governor of Texas and seventh president of Texas A&M University.

Cynthia Ann has many kin, and many descendants, for in accordance with the old customs, Quanah had a family of seven wives. Today, the Oklahoma Parkers and Texas Parkers hold family reunions. They are proud of their heritage. They honor each other's hardships and courage. And many remember this blessing Quanah sent to former foes who named a town for him.

> "May the Great Spirit smile on you.
> May the rains fall in due season
> And in the warmth of sunshine after the rain,
> May the earth yield bountifully.
> May peace and contentment dwell with you
> And your children.
> Forever."

STAGE NOTES

The Squaw with Blue Eyes, in slightly longer form, was premiered at the Backdoor Dinner Theatre in 1982 for the Wichita County Heritage Society as part of its Centennial celebration. In 1983 the author presented it outdoors at Fort Parker for a Parker family reunion of several hundred Indians and Anglos whose ancestors lived this story only a few generations ago. It has also been read in schools, churches, libraries, living rooms, on a front porch on a ranch Comanches once raided, at Quartz Mountain amphitheater in Oklahoma, and in New York.

For small private readings where a log cabin set is impractical, a few country chairs, quilts and baskets will create a mood.

A brief Introduction and Afterword can be shared with the audience by a narrator, or by the actress who plays Cynthia Ann— if special care is taken to move to a different area of the stage.

Music is an asset, particularly the haunting Comanche flute music by Doc Tate Nevaquaya, Comanche painter and musician. Available from Nevaquaya, Box 517, Apache, OK 73006, $11 ppd. by check or money order.

 — The Panhandle — Plains Historical Museum, Canyon, Texas

Cynthia Ann Parker and her daughter,
Prairie Flower, photographed in Fort Worth in
1861 by A.F. Corning shortly after her return
to her Anglo relatives. Her cropped hair is a
Comanche sign of mourning.

Cynthia Ann Parker
1827-1870

Her birth—1827, Illinois

The journey to Texas—1833, 1834

The capture—May 19, 1836

The Indian years—1836-1860

The recapture—December 18, 1860

The daughter's death—1863

Her death—1870, Texas

Her Indian reburial—1910, Oklahoma

—Smithsonian Institution,
National Anthropological Archives, photo 1747-b

Chief Quanah Parker at his home, Star House, in Cache, Oklahoma, with a painting of his mother and sister. Sul Ross, former Texas Ranger, sent him the 1861 photograph, left, and rancher Burk Burnett commissioned the portrait, now in the Parker room at Fort Sill. Photograph 1891 or 1893 by Hutchens/ Lanney.

A defeated Quanah Parker on the reservation after he led the last of the warring Comanches out of the Palo Duro Canyon near what is now Amarillo. Palo Duro, named for its hardwood juniper trees, was a secret campground, a chasm that drops abruptly from the high flat plains. Photograph prior to 1890, Indian Territory/ Oklahoma.

Chief Quanah Parker in Washington, D.C. after he was made a federal judge. He is shown dressed for an official meeting where he represented Comanche, Kiowa, and Apache tribes. By Charles M. Bell, Washington, D.C., circa 1890.

Fort Parker, Cynthia Ann Parker's home as a child in east central Texas, was built of cedar logs. The stockade fence with blockhouse watchtowers was backed inside by two rows of log cabins like the one below, where she and her family lived. Set on a wooded rise in Limestone County near the Navasota, a tributary to the Brazos River, the fort was restored in 1936 and 1967. It is 40 miles east of Waco, between present day Groesbeck and Mexia.

— Log Cabin Village, Fort Worth, Texas

Isaac Parker's log cabin became her home in 1861 when the State Senator returned with his niece to Tarrant County. Originally in Birdville, this dog-trot double log cabin now stands at Log Cabin Village in Fort Worth's Forest Park. Cynthia Ann lived in similar houses in the 1860's with her brother Silas Parker, Jr. in Van Zandt County and with her sister Orlena Parker O'Quinn in Anderson County, where many Anglo Parkers still live.

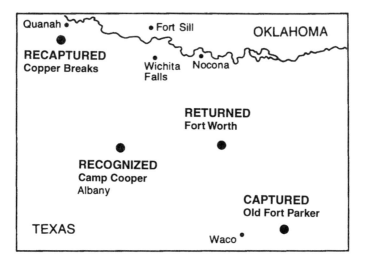

Retracing Cynthia Ann Parker's footsteps

Her trail starts at Fort Parker where she was captured as a nine-year-old child. Near Fort Worth she was returned and reunited with her Parker relatives. Nocona is named for her husband's tribe of Comanches, sometimes called Nokoni, who ranged westward along the Red River beyond the present day town of Quanah. Near Quanah and the Medicine Mounds, is Copper Breaks State Park, which is bordered by the Pease River, site of Cynthia Ann's recapture by Texas Rangers. The neighboring towns, Quanah and Crowell, honor her several times a year. For a schedule of events, write the Chamber of Commerce, P.O. Box 158, Quanah, Texas 79252 or call 817-663-2222. Camp Cooper, where Cynthia Ann was recognized as the lost Parker girl, is no more, though a few ruins are on the legendary Lambshead Ranch. Fort Griffin near Albany, Texas, replaced Cooper after the Civil War and can be visited. For information on Texas forts and state parks, including Old Fort Parker, call 1-800-792-1112. Cynthia Ann's grave is in Oklahoma, at Fort Sill near Lawton and Cache, where many Comanche Parkers live.

"I well remember Cynthia Ann Parker and her little girl," T.C. Cates, a neighbor in Van Zandt County wrote, recalling the early 1860's when she lived there with her brother Silas and his family. "She looked to be stout and weighed about 140 pounds, well-made and liked to work. She had a wild expression and would look down when people looked at her. She could use an ax equal to a man and she liked to work, and disliked a lazy person. She was an expert in tanning hides with hair on them, or plaiting or knitting either ropes or whips. She thought her two boys were lost on the prairie after she was captured and would starve to death. This dissatisfied her very much, and she wanted to go back to the Indians...She was an open-hearted person, good, and always ready to help somebody."

Cynthia Ann Parker's gravestone, photographed at the time of Quanah Parker's death, February 23, 1911, by Bates of Lawton, Oklahoma.

Smithsonian Institution, Photo 45,919

Remembering Cynthia Ann

Cynthia Ann Parker's gravestone is her only place name. It is made of Wichita Mountains red granite, chosen by Quanah who remembered his birthplace as south of that range. Even in death, Cynthia Ann has been an uneasy spirit. She died in east Texas and was buried in the Fosterville Cemetery near Poyner. Chief Quanah, when he felt his own death nearing, wrote to plead with her relatives to let his mother's body be moved. He sent his son-in-law, A.C. Birdsong, to Texas to find the man who had dug her grave and the woman, Mrs. Padgett, who had buttoned a dress and pinned up her hair for her burial. Together they found the unmarked grave and Cynthia Ann was reburied December 3, 1910 at Post Oak Mission Cemetery near Cache, Oklahoma. Quanah had cleaned and washed her bones. Two months later he was buried next to her. His marker is an obelisk of red granite. In the 1930's a reburial service was held for Prairie Flower. In 1957, all three were moved to Chiefs Knoll, Fort Sill Military Post Cemetery, where Prairie Flower's marker is a half-size replica of her mother's; the dates given are 1858-1863.

At Cynthia Ann Parker's service in 1910, Chief Quanah Parker said, "Forty years ago my mother died. She [was] captured by Comanche, nine-years-old. Love Indian and wild life so well she not want to go back to white folks. All same people anyway, God says. I love my mother. I like white people...When end come, then they all be together again."

45

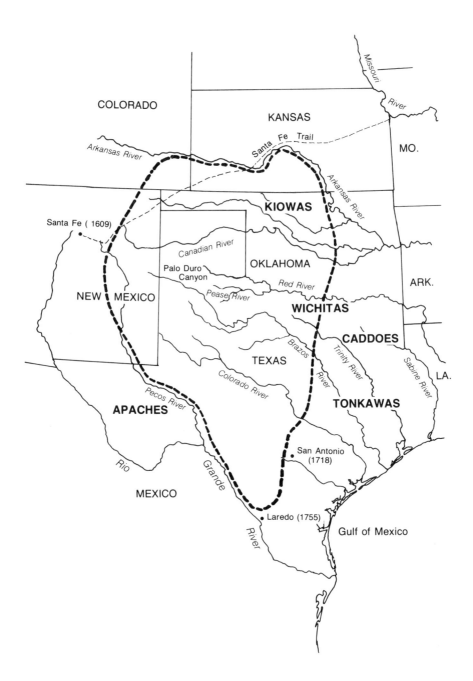

COLORADO

KANSAS

Missouri River

MO.

Santa Fe Trail

Arkansas River

KIOWAS

Arkansas River

Santa Fe (1609)

Canadian River

OKLAHOMA

ARK.

NEW MEXICO

Palo Duro Canyon

Pease River

Red River

WICHITAS

CADDOES

TEXAS

Brazos

Trinity River

Sabine River

LA.

Colorado River

River

APACHES

Pecos River

Rio

San Antonio (1718)

TONKAWAS

Grande

MEXICO

Laredo (1755)

River

Gulf of Mexico

46

The Comanche Lariat

This was the ancestral land of "the lords of the plains." Comanche tribes controlled the southern plains from Kansas to Mexico for most of the 18th and 19th centuries. Their trails, like a giant lariat, encircled some 240,000 square miles, bordered on the north by the Arkansas River, on the west by the Pecos River. Spanish explorers brought horses to the Americas. Comanches mastered the art of riding and of taming wild runaway herds by lassoing and hobbling them, and breathing into their nostrils. At the peak of Comanche prowess it was not unusual for an ordinary brave to own a hundred or more horses. Few white settlements succeeded in this vast area until after the long struggle and final surrender of the Quahadi, Chief Quanah's tribe, in 1875.